NBA CHAMPIONSHIPS:

↓

NONE

↓

ALL-TIME LEADING SCORER:

↓

DWIGHT HOWARD (2004–12):

↓

11,435 POINTS

THE NBA: A HISTORY OF HOOPS

ORLANDO MAGIC

BY JIM WHITING

CREATIVE EDUCATION   CREATIVE PAPERBACKS

Published by Creative Education
and Creative Paperbacks

P.O. Box 227, Mankato, Minnesota 56002

Creative Education and Creative Paperbacks
are imprints of The Creative Company

www.thecreativecompany.us

Design by Blue Design; production by Joe Kahnke

Printed in the United States of America

Photographs by Alamy (stephen searle), Corbis
(Michael Martin/NewSport), Getty Images (Doug
Benc/Stringer/Getty Images Sport, Andrew D.
Bernstein/NBAE, Nathaniel S. Butler/NBAE, Vince
Compagnone/Los Angeles Times, Elsa/Getty
Images Sport, Andy Hayt/NBAE, Jon Hayt/NBAE,
Fernando Medina/NBAE, Orlando Sentinel/
Tribune News Service, Tom Pidgeon/ Stringer/
Getty Images Sport, TONY RANZE/Stringer/
AFP, The Sporting News, Mark J. Terrill-Pool/
Getty Images Sport), Newscom (St. Petersburg
Times/ZUMA PRESS, ERIK S. LESSER/EPA)

Library of Congress Cataloging-in-Publication Data

Names: Whiting, Jim, 1943- author.

Title: Orlando Magic / Jim Whiting.

Series: The NBA: A History of Hoops.

Includes bibliographical references and index.

Summary: This high-interest title summarizes
the history of the Orlando Magic professional
basketball team, highlighting memorable events
and noteworthy players such as Dwight Howard.

Identifiers: LCCN 2017006897 / ISBN 978-1-60818-
856-7 (hardcover) / ISBN 978-1-62832-459-4
(pbk) / ISBN 978-1-56660-904-3 (eBook)

Subjects: LCSH: 1. Orlando Magic (Basketball
team)—History—Juvenile literature.
2. Orlando Magic (Basketball team)—
Biography—Juvenile literature.

Classification: LCC GV885.52.O75 W445 2017 /
DDC 796.323/640975924—dc23

CCSS: RI.4.1, 2, 3, 4; RI.5.1, 2, 4; RI.6.1, 2,
3; RF.4.3, 4; RF.5.3, 4; RH. 6-8. 4, 5, 7

First Edition HC 9 8 7 6 5 4 3 2 1

First Edition PBK 9 8 7 6 5 4 3 2 1

CONTENTS

LEGENDS OF THE HARDWOOD

8

Situated in central Florida,
is famous for its theme parks, including
Walt Disney World's Epcot Center.

MAKING MAGIC

any National
Basketball Association (NBA) fans wanted the Cleveland
Cavaliers to play the Los Angeles Lakers in the 2009
Finals. The teams had the league's best records. It would
be a classic matchup between two superstars: LeBron
James of the Cavaliers and Kobe Bryant of the Lakers.

Center **DWIGHT HOWARD** and the Magic overcame the Cavaliers to reach the Finals in 2009.

The Orlando Magic had other ideas. They had their own superstar in Dwight Howard. They defeated the defending champion Boston Celtics in the Eastern Conference semifinals. Then Orlando faced the Cavaliers. The Magic won Game 1 by a single point. They won Game 4 by two points to lead the series. Cleveland came back to win Game 5. Howard and his teammates bolted to a 58–40 halftime lead in Game 6. The Magic cruised to a 103–90 win. Howard had 40 points. James had 25. "This team has fought really, really hard," said Orlando coach Stan Van Gundy. "Our reward is you get to go from preparing for LeBron to preparing for Kobe." The NBA still had a classic matchup for the championship. It was Disney World vs. Disneyland. Florida Mickey Mouse vs. California Mickey Mouse.

n 1986, Orlando civic officials wanted an NBA franchise. They thought having a team name already picked out would help their

MASCOT MAGIC

A few months before the Magic started playing games, a large "egg" exploded in front of the Orlando Arena. A fuzzy green dragon emerged. This was Stuff the Magic Dragon. He is the official mascot of the Magic. His name is a spin on the 1960s song, "Puff the Magic Dragon." "Stuff" also means slam dunk. Stuff is one of the NBA's most famous mascots. He performs at community events as well as games. Every year he hosts the Celebrity Mascot Games. The event raises money for the New Hope for Kids charity. "We could not be happier with Stuff," said Magic official Cari Haught. "He's lovable, he's funny, he's full of surprises."

chances. They held a name-the-team contest in a local newspaper. The top choice was Challengers. It honored the memory of the *Challenger* space shuttle. The shuttle had exploded earlier that year shortly after takeoff. A panel of judges didn't like that idea, though. They chose Magic instead. The panel said the name refers to "the magic of Orlando—a tourist hotspot with lots to offer visitors." The city's main attraction is Disney World. Other destinations include Universal Studios, SeaWorld, Gatorland, and Wet 'n Wild Water Park.

13

rlando received its franchise the following year. The Magic began playing in the 1989–90 season. The team lived up to its nickname in the first preseason game. The "new kids on the block" defeated the defending NBA champion Detroit Pistons 118–109. "We thought *we* were the defending champions after that game," said Magic

Forward **DENNIS SCOTT** earned the nickname "3-D" for his long-range shooting.

guard Morlon Wiley. A month into the season, Orlando had a 7–7 record. It was the best start by an expansion team. But the Magic finished with an 18–64 record. Scoring wasn't the problem. Orlando had the fifth-highest point total in the league. But the Magic gave up more points than anyone else.

Orlando improved to 31–51 in its second season. Scrappy point guard Scott Skiles was named the league's Most Improved Player. He set an NBA single-game assist record of 30. "If any of those shots were missed, I would have fallen short, so I owe the record to my teammates," he said. Another record-setter was rookie forward Dennis Scott. He sank 125 three-pointers during the season. It was the best-ever long-distance performance by a rookie.

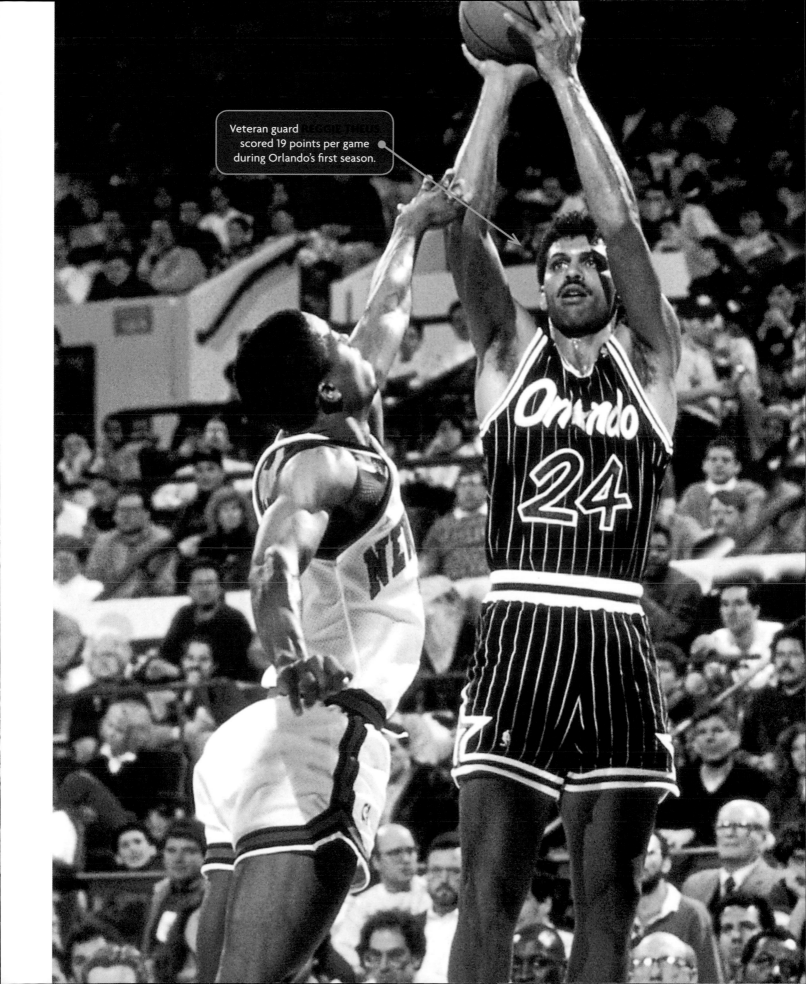

Veteran guard **REGGIE THEUS** scored 19 points per game during Orlando's first season.

Massive center **SHAQUILLE O'NEAL** led the NBA in scoring in 1994–95.

SHAQ ATTACK

The Magic took a step backward in 1991–92. Several key players were injured. At one point, Orlando suffered a 17-game losing streak. Its final mark was a dismal 21–61. But there was a silver lining. The poor record led to the top pick in the 1992 NBA Draft. Orlando chose 7-foot-1 and 300-pound center

"THERE'S NO DOUBT HE'S GOING TO BE A MONSTER. HE PALMS THE BALL LIKE A GRAPEFRUIT."

Shaquille O'Neal. "There's no doubt he's going to be a monster," said Miami Heat center Rony Seikaly. "He palms the ball like a grapefruit." "Shaq" lived up to expectations. He averaged more than 23 points, 13 rebounds, and 3 blocked shots per game. He was an obvious choice as Rookie of the Year. He helped the team win 41 games. Orlando almost made the playoffs.

The Magic added rookie point guard Anfernee "Penny" Hardaway in a draft-day trade the following year. Though he stood 6-foot-7, Hardaway played point guard. His height gave him an advantage over the league's other point guards. He and O'Neal formed one of the best inside-outside combinations in the NBA. "I'm glad I'm getting out of this game soon," said longtime Los Angeles Lakers forward James Worthy. "I don't want to be around when those two grow up." Orlando surged to

O'NEAL'S high-powered dunking broke two backboards during his rookie season.

19

20

A PRETTY PENNY

ANFERNEE "PENNY" HARDAWAY, POINT GUARD, 6-FOOT-7, 1993–99

Orlando had the top overall draft choice in 1993. It planned on taking power forward Chris Webber. Penny Hardaway hadn't impressed team officials. But he had impressed Shaq. Shaq called team officials. "You guys need to bring [Penny] down again," he said. "I promise you need to take a better look." Hardaway impressed everyone this time. "I didn't really miss a shot, I had some unbelievable assists finding guys all throughout the day, on the fast break I pushed the ball every single time," he said. The Magic drafted Webber. They immediately traded him for Hardaway and three first-round draft picks. Magic fans were upset—until they saw Hardaway in action.

a 50–32 mark. The team made the playoffs for the first time. Though the Indiana Pacers swept Orlando in the first round, the future was bright.

Orlando's fortune glowed in 1994–95. In just their sixth season, the Magic won 57 games. That was the best record in the Eastern Conference! Orlando defeated the Celtics, the Chicago Bulls, and the Pacers to reach the Finals. There it faced the defending champion Houston Rockets. The Rockets featured their own dominating center, 7-foot-tall Hakeem Olajuwon. His last-second tip-in gave Houston the victory in Game 1. The Rockets won the next three as well, clinching the championship for the second year in a row.

Orlando did even better in the following season. It won 60 games. Scott was one reason for the team's continued success. He set an NBA record by sinking 267 three-point shots. The Magic swept the Pistons in

22

Superstars Michael Jordan and O'Neal faced each other many times on the court during the 1990s.

the first round of the playoffs. They defeated the Atlanta Hawks, four

games to one, in the second round. Then they faced Chicago in the

Eastern Conference finals. Bulls superstar Michael Jordan had returned to

the team after playing baseball for two years. He helped power Chicago

to a 72–10 season. At the time, it was the most regular-season wins in

NBA history. The Magic fell as the Bulls swept the series.

LEGENDS OF THE HARDWOOD

FOUR ON THE FLOOR

1995 NBA FINALS, HOUSTON ROCKETS VS. ORLANDO MAGIC, GAME 1, JUNE 7, 1995

Ten seconds remained. Orlando led by three. Guard Nick Anderson had two foul shots. A Magic win was virtually guaranteed. TV announcer Marv Albert commented, "Nick Anderson ... usually a dependable free throw shooter." This night, he wasn't. Both shots clanged off the rim. Anderson grabbed the second miss. He was fouled again. Again Anderson missed both. Houston sank a three-pointer to force overtime. The Rockets won 120–118 and went on to sweep the series. Anderson still works for the Magic as a well-liked and popular team official. One night he went to a restaurant. The waitress said, "I called my boyfriend and told him you were here. He wants to know why you missed those four free throws."

After **O'NEAL** left Orlando, the Magic—and the rest of the NBA—struggled to keep up with him.

O'NEAL MOVES ON

Losing to the Bulls wasn't Orlando's only setback. O'Neal became a free agent after the season. That meant he could play anywhere he wanted. The Magic offered him a huge contract.

"WHEN I WAS IN ORLANDO, I REALLY FELT LIKE A BIG FISH IN A SMALL, DRIED-UP POND. NO MATTER WHAT I DID, IT GOT TALKED ABOUT, UNTIL I COULDN'T REALLY LIVE MY LIFE."

He chose to go to the Lakers instead. Money was one reason. He would also get more media attention in California. And he wanted to maintain some privacy, too. "When I was in Orlando, I really felt like a big fish in a small, dried-up pond," he said. "No matter what I did, it got talked about, until I couldn't really live my life. But out in L.A., for everything you do, there's always some other star acting crazier."

26

Rony Seikaly did his best to replace O'Neal at center. But Hardaway was injured. He missed more than 20 games. The Magic still managed to win 45 games. They faced the Miami Heat in the first round of the playoffs. The Heat easily won the first two games. Hardaway scored more than 40 points in each of the next two games. Orlando won both of them. In Game 5, Miami clung to a 3-point lead with 14 seconds left. Hardaway drained a three-pointer. Unfortunately, it

Center **RONY SEIKALY** led the Magic with 9.5 rebounds per game in 1996–97.

28

T-MAC'S BIG NIGHT

TRACY McGRADY, SHOOTING GUARD/SMALL FORWARD, 6-FOOT-8, 2000–04

Tracy McGrady had just seven points in the first quarter against the Washington Wizards on March 10, 2004. Then he scored 45 points in the next 2 quarters. "It was just one of those nights where he had it going," said Wizards coach Eddie Jordan. Fans hoped he would "go" to 70 points. Only four players had ever scored that many. But he missed 10 of 11 shots and 9 free throws in the fourth quarter. "It was in the back of my mind, that's why I was missing free throws," he said. "That's why I went on a little cold drought missing jumpers, layups, because I was thinking about it." He still finished with 62 points.

was *Tim* Hardaway of the Heat, not *Penny* of the Magic. Miami went on to win, 91–83. Orlando's season was over.

After splitting the 1997–98 season 41–41, the Magic returned to the playoffs the following season. Again they made an early exit as they lost to the Philadelphia 76ers. Penny Hardaway asked to be traded. Without him, most experts predicted that the Magic would have a terrible season. New coach Glenn "Doc" Rivers didn't listen to the experts. His players listened to him. While Orlando had another 41–41 season, it was much better than expected. Rivers was named Coach of the Year. The team missed the playoffs by just one game.

rlando signed explosive swingman Tracy McGrady the following season. The team also drafted sharpshooting guard/forward Mike Miller. Both moves paid off. Miller was named

Swingman **TRACY McGRADY** filled highlight reels with his soaring dunks and high-scoring games.

30

Rookie of the Year. McGrady was voted the league's Most Improved Player. The Magic won 43 games and returned to the playoffs. They lost to the Milwaukee Bucks in the first round. The pattern was virtually identical in the next two seasons. After winning the opening game of the 2003–04 season, Orlando fell apart. The Magic lost 19 games in a row. Rivers was fired halfway through the streak. At 21–61, it was the worst record in the NBA that season. McGrady provided one of the few bright spots. He became the second-youngest player to reach 10,000 points in his career. Only Kobe Bryant reached that level more quickly. But, faced with the prospect of more losses in Orlando, T-Mac asked for a trade.

The fifth pick overall in the 2000 NBA Draft, **MIKE MILLER** earned Rookie of the Year honors.

Drafted straight from high school, **HOWARD** became a six-time All-Star in Orlando.

ANOTHER SUPERSTAR ARRIVES

Once again, a poor finish paved the way for Orlando to draft a future superstar. This time it was 6-foot-11 center Dwight Howard. He won several awards as the nation's top high school player.

Howard chose not to attend college. He entered the 2004 Draft instead. His idol, Kevin Garnett of the Minnesota Timberwolves, had done the same thing in 1995. Howard even chose his number (12) by reversing the digits of Garnett's 21. He became the first player to start all 82 regular-season NBA games straight out of high school. Howard finished with averages of 12 points and 10 rebounds a game. He was chosen for the All-Rookie first team. Orlando added point guard Jameer Nelson in the same draft. The Magic improved to 36 wins. "We've got something to look forward to next year," said Howard. "Next year" wasn't as successful as he had hoped. The Magic won 16 of their last 22 games to just barely match the previous year's total of 36 wins.

rlando improved to 40 wins in 2006–07. It squeaked into the playoffs. Detroit swept the Magic in the first round.

As of 2017, HOWARD still held many Magic records, including points, blocks, and total rebounds.

During his single season in Orlando, guard _____ boosted the Magic to the playoffs.

> "WE'VE HAD A GOOD SEASON, BUT WE KNOW WE HAVE TO WIN IN THE PLAYOFFS TO GET A LITTLE MORE RESPECT."

With Howard continuing to improve and the addition of several new faces, the Magic won 52 games the following season. It was their best mark in 11 years. Forward Hedo Turkoglu was named the league's Most Improved Player. "We've had a good season," said forward Rashard Lewis, one of the newcomers, "but we know we have to win in the playoffs to get a little more respect." They did. The Magic romped past the Toronto Raptors, four games to one. That broke a streak of seven straight playoff series losses. "To finally get over the hump and get out of the first round, it means a lot," said Howard. But again the Pistons ended the Magic's season. Orlando won just a single game in the series.

The Magic fired on all cylinders the following season. They won 59 games. Nelson was injured in midseason. Team officials quickly traded for speedy guard Rafer Alston to fill in for him. He proved

38

A MAGIC MOMENT

2009 EASTERN CONFERENCE FINALS, CLEVELAND CAVALIERS AT ORLANDO MAGIC, MAY 30, 2009

The teams came back on the court after halftime. Dwight Howard was practicing his free throw shooting before play resumed. Cleveland center Lorenzen Wright was hurt and wasn't playing. He wore a business suit instead of his uniform. He walked to the basket where Howard was shooting and watched him. He wanted to throw Howard off his rhythm. Wright jumped up and grabbed the net. He tried to swat the ball away. The ball rose up into the air and then dropped back through the hoop. It seemed symbolic of the magic Orlando generated to defeat the Cavaliers in the series.

Guard **RAFER ALSTON** joined the Magic late in 2008–09 and boosted the team to the Finals.

an ideal fit to run the offense. At the other end of the court, Howard won the first of three straight Defensive Player of the Year awards. Orlando swept through the Eastern Conference playoffs. They faced the Lakers for the NBA championship. Los Angeles easily won the first game. The next three were close. Orlando managed to win one of them. The Magic hosted Game 5. But even the home crowd didn't help. Howard scored just 11 points. Los Angeles took the championship with a 99–86 win. "Look at it, just see how they're celebrating," Howard said. "It should motivate us to want to get in the gym, want to get better."

40

TIME TO REBUILD

T he Magic won 59 games again in 2009–10. They swept their first two playoff series. They faced the Celtics in the conference finals. Orlando lost the first two games at home by a total of seven points.

Sharpshooting guard **VINCE CARTER** helped Orlando reach 59 wins in 2009–10.

ASSISTING ORLANDO

SCOTT SKILES, POINT GUARD, 6-FOOT-1, 1989–94; COACH, 2015–16

Scott Skiles was an original member of the Magic. He held the team record for assists until Jameer Nelson arrived. Skiles was known for his intense, gritty style of play. "I played more of a tough kind of game," he said. "That was the only way I could play in order to survive and have a career." Skiles brought the same intensity as coach. "We have a defensive system we teach and work on every day," Skiles said. "It can be tedious to have to do the drill work every day and stay with it." Power forward Andrew Nicholson added, "There is a lot more discipline.... We're just playing the right way."

LEGENDS OF THE HARDWOOD

> "ARE WE TAKING A STEP BACK?
> ABSOLUTELY, WE ARE. BUT WE'RE
> TAKING A STEP BACK WITH A VISION."

The Celtics strode to an easy win in Game 3. Orlando's season seemed to be over. No team had ever come back from a 3–0 series deficit. Orlando came close. It won the next two games. But Boston burst out to a 30–19 first-quarter lead in Game 6. The Celtics coasted to a series-ending 96–84 win. "It seemed like whoever was the most aggressive in the first quarter throughout the series won the games," said Nelson. "[It] kind of set the tone. It's tough, nobody wants it to end." Orlando dropped to 52 wins the following season. It quickly exited the playoffs.

The 2011–12 season started late because of a players' strike. That wasn't the only problem. Nearly the entire season was a "Dwightmare." Howard didn't think team officials were doing enough to build a championship team. He kept asking to be traded. It was a big distraction. Orlando still compiled a 37–29 mark. Though they made the playoffs, the Magic lost to the Pacers in the first round. Howard got his wish after the season. Orlando received six new players and several draft choices. "Are we taking a step back?" said general manager Rob Hennigan. "Absolutely, we are. But we're taking a step back with a vision." That "vision" wasn't immediately clear. The "step back" was. Orlando plunged to 20–62. It was the team's worst record since its first season more than 20 years earlier. The Magic didn't do much better in the following two seasons. They won 23 games in 2013–14 and 25 in 2014–15.

43

44

The Magic rebounded in 2015–16 when Skiles returned as coach. They won 35 games. They still didn't make the playoffs. That was the longest dry spell since the team's first four years. Orlando continued to rebuild. A key piece was 7-foot center Nikola Vucevic. He added scoring and rebounding punch. Another was small forward Evan Fournier. At 23, he was in his fourth NBA season. He began his pro career in his native France as a teenager. "I was already the leading scorer of my French team the year before I got drafted [in 2012 by the Denver Nuggets]. It was my first time being the leader of a team, and it's helping me now." The Magic could have used a lot of help in 2016–17. They dipped to 29 wins. And 16 of their 53 losses were by 20 points or more. A preseason trade for power forward Serge Ibaka didn't work out. He was traded away during the season.

In a city built on dreams, the Orlando Magic have provided plenty of real-world rewards for their fans. More often than not, the team has found its way into the playoffs. Fans hope that the team's crop of young players will mature and lead the Magic back to the NBA Finals.

Center **NIKOLA VUCEVIC** grabbed a franchise-record 29 rebounds in a 2012 game against the Heat.

SELECTED BIBLIOGRAPHY

Ballard, Chris. *The Art of a Beautiful Game: The Thinking Fan's Tour of the NBA*. New York: Simon & Schuster, 2010.

Hareas, John. *Ultimate Basketball: More Than 100 Years of the Sport's Evolution*. New York: DK, 2004.

Hubbard, Jan, ed. *The Official NBA Basketball Encyclopedia*. 3rd edition. New York: Doubleday, 2000.

NBA.com. "Orlando Magic." http://www.nba.com/magic/.

Simmons, Bill. *The Book of Basketball: The NBA According to the Sports Guy*. New York: Ballantine, 2009.

Sports Illustrated. *Sports Illustrated Basketball's Greatest*. New York: Sports Illustrated, 2014.

WEBSITES

JR. NBA

http://jr.nba.com/

This kids site has games, videos, game results, team and player information, statistics, and more.

SHAQ SHOWS UP FOR EPIC BASKETBALL GAME WITH KIDS

https://www.youtube.com/watch?v=MhBH5IM5gic

After a Florida police officer responds to a noise complaint by playing basketball with some young people, he challenges them to a rematch—and brings "backup."

Note: Every effort has been made to ensure that any websites listed above were active at the time of publication. However, because of the nature of the Internet, it is impossible to guarantee that these sites will remain active indefinitely or that their contents will not be altered.

INDEX